On Tuesdays We Are WILD

Mindfulness Adventures with Microwave Bling Bling

Cynthia Berenyi

MINDFULNESS MERMAID PUBLISHING

Cynthia Berenyi

On Tuesdays We Are Wild:
Mindfulness Adventures with Microwave Bling Bling

Mindfulness Mermaid Publishing

Editor: Lori Bamber
Proofreader: Elise Volkman

Illustrators: Kevin Isaac & Stephen Mason
Cover & Text Design: Kristy Twellmann Hill

For 2022-2023 DIV 3 class, who all inspired this book and who showed me how magical moments and microwaves can be.

For my mother, who always supports me and my writing journey.

For my father, who supports me from above and who is always in my heart.

For my grandparents, who are always with me and remind me to be mindful.

For all those teachers, especially Lisa Baylis and Stephanie Curran, who taught me about mindfulness, especially when I was reluctant to learn, and when I needed mindfulness the most.

For everyone who has ever had an emotion, and for everyone who wishes to understand themselves and their emotions better.

What if—with just a push of a button—a reset button—you could pause and feel calm inside at any time?

Chapter One
Johnny

It seemed like a typical Tuesday in Ms. T's grade 4/5 class.

It was far from a typical Tuesday, but we didn't know that yet.

It was lunch time, and I stood in the microwave line to warm up my food—delicious macaroni with cheese that looked at me through the see-through glass container my mom packed it in.

Only Michael and Jenni were in front of me, so I knew it wouldn't be long, but I felt a vibration bubbling up inside of me because I had to wait. My heart raced and my body began to feel like it was fighting me on the inside.

Not unusual. I had a little body for a person in grade 4/5, but the pressure inside me made me feel like I was enormous. My mind began to wander, which is something that happens a lot. Mind wandering is a coping tool. Although it isn't really a coping tool. Mind wandering makes things even worse sometimes, but it does help me escape the feelings going on inside my body.

Standing there with my leftover macaroni in my hand, I began to think, to daydream, to get lost in my thoughts.

Tuesdays always felt chaotic, and what that means is us students were always wild.

I don't know what it was about Tuesdays.

I don't know if it was because Ms. T always said we were wild on Tuesdays and that made us wild, or if there was something weird about Tuesdays.

Sometimes I think we are wild because Ms. T says we are—maybe we want her to be right. Maybe she should instead say how calm we are on Tuesdays!

This Tuesday morning, when she was trying to read a story and we wouldn't stop talking, Ms. T said it again—and we all laughed in the crazy wild way we only seem to laugh on Tuesdays. Ms. T is usually really happy and always positive, but I think that there is something about Tuesdays that makes her question all of her life decisions. I think this because I am a kid who thinks about everything: not only my emotions, but other people's emotions, deep in my body. Sometimes it can be very, very, very over-whelming and I don't know what to do in those situations.

Sometimes I have so much energy in my body that I have to throw myself to the ground to try and make it stop. Sometimes people stare at me, and that makes me feel worse. I have been trying to push these emotions down and away my whole life, but they always come to the surface, no matter how hard I try to ignore them or to pretend I do not have them.

Ms. T tries to teach me and the class about our emotions, and I do believe that helps me. Well, a little bit. She talks about recognizing the emotions through the feelings that come up in our bodies first, and recognizing the emotions as soon as they begin to change from a grounded level of zero, to a level above the ground, up the emotion tree.

Climbing trees can be fun, but not when you get

up so high that you cannot see the ground.

Ms. T lets us know that feeling all of the emotions is part of being human, and when we can recognize our emotions in the moment without judgment, we can find tools to help us use our parachute to have a safe landing back to feeling grounded.

Ms. T always asks us to tell her what feeling grounded feels like, looks like, and sounds like. She tells us that the more we are aware of what feeling grounded is for us, the easier it can be to come back to this state. Feeling grounded is when you feel balanced, safe and centered inside yourself. You are mindful and in the present moment. You are aware if your mind wanders into the past or the future, giving you the ability to gently bring yourself back to the present moment.

You are exactly where you are, exactly as you are. Your feet are on the ground, roots are growing, creating connections to the earth, self, and others—a connection to all things. When you feel grounded there are happy, calm, easeful, and steady feelings. It is in feeling grounded where you can be aware of all of your emotions and feelings without losing control.

An emotion tree contains all of the emotions. When your feelings take you up the emotion tree it can be challenging to see your connections to the earth, self, and others.

I don't usually recognize when my emotions begin to climb up the emotion tree. Ms. T reassures me that it is an ongoing journey and that we are all always learning. She reassures me that whatever I am experiencing is okay, but I just don't know if I believe that. I usually only notice my emotions when I am at the top of the tree, on a tiny, wobbly branch, inside my anger, and then it is too late—I am out of control.

Feeling grounded is a new feeling for me, that I am learning how to recognize. I don't know if I am doing a good job, as feeling grounded feels strange to me.

I guess sometimes I do feel grounded, but it doesn't seem to be that often.

Ms. T often talks about having tools in our emotional backpacks. I can use my tools and open my backpack into a parachute, which makes it easy to glide back down to a grounded feeling. It feels like I need my backpack of tools every day. Maybe that is okay, but I don't know.

It makes me feel sick in my stomach just thinking about all this stuff, stuff I usually think about all the time. My body usually feels like it is ready for something to happen. It is like my body is a guard, trying to protect me, always ready to fight, run or hide. (Ms. T calls that "fight, flight, or freeze mode," which she says is just the brain's way to protect us from danger or the idea of danger.)

Even though I get that my brain and body are trying to protect me, it makes me feel trapped. I don't know how to tell my brain and body that I don't need them to protect me, that I am safe.

Part of me doesn't even know if I am ever really safe. What if my body is right and the thoughts that I am safe are wrong? I am always wondering about that. Am I safe, am I not safe? It is absolutely exhausting.

But this is the only way I know how to be.

One emotional backpack tool my teacher doesn't know about is our class microwave.

I don't know what it is about that microwave, but it helps me feel calm and makes me smile. Someone in the class put googly eyes and a paper mouth on it. I know that it is an object and it is not alive, but sometimes, I swear, it smiles at me.

Sometimes it just looks right at me with those googly eyes and I feel seen and accepted for exactly who I am.

I sometimes wonder if other kids feel the same way, because our class even gave the microwave a name: Microwave Bling Bling. I don't know why we call it that. Maybe because of the sounds it makes, but those sounds are more like a beep, beep.

Our class also named an eraser Kevin. Kevin got married to another eraser named Linda. The whole class acts like these objects and school supplies are alive, and our teacher doesn't tell us otherwise. In fact, she organized the whole eraser wedding and the naming of the microwave.

"Johnny, Johnny, Johnny," I could hear in the background of my thoughts.

Jenni, who had yummy chicken that I could smell through the Tupperware container she just warmed up, was finished using the microwave and began pulling my arm forward.

"Let me go NOW!" I yelled.

Jenni dropped my arm and hunched her shoulders as her smile transformed into a frown.

I was startled, because I was so lost in my thoughts that I had no idea what was going on in real life, right in front of me, or why someone was pulling me. The pulling of my arm scared me.

"I was just trying to help you and tell you I was done with the microwave," Jenni said gently as she quietly walked away.

I stuck my tongue out at her, as it was all I could think to do.

I didn't even know what had just happened. Sometimes my daydreams can take me out of life so far, like this time; I didn't know where I was or even who I was, and I was lost. Then, that look happened, the one I knew so well—the look of disappointment.

I really care about people, like Jenni. Jenni is so sweet. She never yells back at me, but, at times, she creates distance between us. Which is probably smart, because sometimes when I feel like I've disappointed someone, I do things to disappoint them more.

Being honest about my feelings scares me too much. No way am I going to share my inside feelings, no way, no how, no thank you.

Instead, I do or say things that could be thought of as mean, like sticking my tongue out (which isn't the worst thing I have done).

"Um, Johnny, are you going to use the microwave?" Chelsea asked behind me.

"Yes," I huffed under my breath as I stomped my feet loudly while moving toward the microwave.

I didn't realize I was stomping. I didn't realize I was about to do any of the actions my body chose to do next. It was almost like a darkness came over me, and I was completely out of it, climbing high up the emotion tree. My hands turned into fists and my shoulders inched far up toward my ears. My teeth clenched, my face scrunched up and my eyes squinted with anger, embarrassment and disappointment. My hands slammed my container on top of the microwave. I jumped back, surprising myself at the loud bang it made. I opened the microwave door and it swung open with a great force, my great force, which almost caused it to break.

The microwave was hot!

It radiated so much heat, much like my body felt all over. I was sweating and warm and my face felt

like it was on fire with embarrassment and anger.

Maybe the microwave was angry too—was Microwave Bling Bling disappointed in me too?

Thinking about that was too much for me to handle. I couldn't imagine the microwave being disappointed in me, the one thing I felt actually cared for me. I know that seems stupid, but it was true.

I was lost in all my thoughts and ready to scream, and as I pushed the microwave's reset button, the microwave screamed instead.

Bling. ZIP. ZAP. ZOOP. POOF. KABAM. BEEP!

The microwave's lights shut off and there was no power. The paper smile didn't change into a sad face, but it seemed that the microwave's mouth turned down and was frowning.

This had happened once before, and we could not use the microwave for days until some people from another place came to fix it.

I couldn't think, I couldn't feel, and everything went even more black and numb. I was in a nightmare now, a terrible nightmare, far up the emotion tree.

I screamed, "NOOOOOOOOOO," and fell to the ground.

My glass container with macaroni fell to the carpet beside my body, the glass breaking into a million pieces, much like my heart. I rolled on the ground and began slamming my fists into the carpet as I continued to yell "NOOOOO," over and over.

"Okay, everyone, the microwave isn't working. Please stay away from this area while we sort this out," Ms. T announced to the class.

She looked over at me and reached out her hand. "Johnny, please be careful. How about we get you up off the floor away from the glass?"

I held my hand out but then pulled it right back, embarrassed and angry. I was right by Jenni's desk. I looked up at her from the floor. Even with all of this happening around her, Jenni looked so quiet and calm. How could she be so calm? Maybe she was so calm because she was able to warm her food up.

I was mad at her.

She looked down at me and her eyes widened. For a moment, she looked scared. She looked like she wanted to raise her hand, but couldn't.

I wish I could be like her, not dealing with all of these emotions.

"I hate you," I yelled at her, and then ran out of the classroom screaming it over and over again at the top of my lungs.

Ms. T followed me out into the hallway.

Chapter 2

Jenni

Ms. T walked back into the classroom and said, "Johnny just needs a minute in the hall. Can we respect that and give him some space?"

The class nodded in agreement.

Ms. T looked at me and said, "Jenni, do you want to say something?"

How had she known I wanted to say something? I wanted to say something, but it was hard for me to raise my hand or bring myself to speak, especially in front of adults. I felt scared to share my feelings and I knew I had to be respectful of other people. How could I respect myself and my feelings, and respect others and their feelings at the same time?

It was a mystery.

Ms. T leaned down toward me and whispered to be careful of the broken glass by my desk.

"Is Johnny okay?" I was finally able to say.

"Yes, he will be. Thank you for asking about Johnny. Asking about others is a kind gesture and shows you are a caring friend," Ms. T responded.

I smiled. But underneath that smile, I knew that I wasn't a caring friend to myself. In the background of all my thoughts and feelings, parts of me did not like myself. My eyes began to dart back and forth, and my breathing became a bit short and heavy.

Ms. T stayed close and asked, "Now, how are you? Are you doing alright?"

I really wanted to say the truth: "I am scared and I would like a hug." But my voice started shaking even at the thought of asking for what I needed. I felt my body wiggle a little bit. A giggle came out of my mouth, and I have no idea why.

"I am f-fine," I stammered, somehow managing to get some words out.

"I am here if you need anything," said Ms. T. "If you need to talk, a hug, or to open the window and get some fresh air—just let me know what you need."

I wanted to tell her that I needed a hug, but I couldn't. It wasn't her job to give me a hug. She was my teacher. It felt like no one ever gave me what I needed, but I also didn't know how to ask for what I needed, so I couldn't be angry at anyone. I saved all the anger for myself.

Ms. T began to pick up some of the glass that had punctured its way into the carpet around my desk. It was mixed with macaroni and dirt, and it was all a big mess. Some other students asked if they could help, and they got the garbage can and paper towel for Ms. T.

I wish I had offered to help, but I was too nervous. I felt a huge rush of energy going up and down my spine. It felt like a rollercoaster, up my back and down my back, up and down, up and down—I was on the rollercoaster, trying not to scream.

I tried to put my hand up to ask for help, but then my hand came down. It was hopeless. Even if some-one noticed my hand, no words could come out of my mouth.

As Ms. T cleaned up the glass, some of the other kids asked about Johnny.

I couldn't stop thinking about him either. Johnny was one of my best friends, but maybe he didn't know that. I had never told him. I barely talked— only if I had to. I really liked Johnny and it worried me that he wasn't in class. I was worried about everything. I worried that I got to warm up my food and Johnny didn't. I wished I could have traded our spots in line. I wished the microwave had stayed alive.

What would have happened if it did?

What will happen if it never comes back to life?

That microwave was a solid part of our class. We used it every day. Maybe it got tired of just giving, giving, giving and us taking, taking, taking. We were never really thankful. We just expected it to always work. I know the microwave isn't alive, but I worry about its feelings too. Could it have feelings?

What if the microwave had so many feelings too, but was afraid to say anything, like me?

The thought made my rollercoaster energy relax. Our microwave reminded me I wasn't so alone.

Ms. T managed to clean all the glass we could see and one of my classmates, Michael, helped to put up the chairs and made signs to keep people off the carpet, in case there were invisible bits left. Ms. T smiled and thanked everyone for the help.

Michael was always helpful, always social. He was sometimes sad, but everyone liked him. He was able to share his feelings and say what he wanted. Standing by my desk, he looked so confident. How could he be so confident and social? I was envious of him.

He looked over at me, and I felt like he could see right through me, as if he knew I was thinking about him, comparing myself to him. My heart raced and the energy shot up and down my spine again. My body shook and my face began to feel hot. I was embarrassed and afraid that someone would say something to me, so I put my head down and rested it on my desk. I could still see a bit through my hands. I watched Michael secretively as he walked away to the other side of the room to play with his friends.

Ms. T followed him and the other kids and I watched Michael and her laughing about something.

Chapter 3

Michael

"You always have the funniest jokes, Michael! Where do you come up with this stuff?" Ms. T laughed and laughed, and then I laughed and laughed. Charlotte, Jayde, Marlee, Max, and Henry all laughed too.

"I like when you say, 'They were soooooo far out.' The way you say that line is the funny part of the joke. Sometimes you do such good impressions!" Ms. T told me.

"Thank you," I replied. My eyes lit up and beamed with joy. Other kids gathered around me, and we all started telling jokes and laughing. It lightened the mood and that is what we needed after the microwave incident. I felt like it was my job to lighten the mood and make sure everyone was okay. I mean, I know it wasn't my responsibility to do that—maybe it was Ms. T's responsibility or our own responsibility—but I always felt like it was mine.

That is why I always told jokes and sometimes did magic tricks. But I was getting tired. I felt like a machine, always performing on demand, but I also wanted everyone to like me, so I had to keep going.

My magic tricks were good. No one could figure out how I had found their card in the pile. But as soon as I told one joke or did one trick, people wanted new jokes and new magic tricks. I just couldn't keep up.

As soon as Charlotte asked, "Hey, do you know any new ones?" my shoulders felt incredibly heavy and I felt the light in my eyes being blown out like a birthday candle.

My heart and smile dropped into a frown. My heart was frowning. Do you know how that felt? It felt incredibly sad. The saddest feeling of sad.

Ms. T walked by and said, "Michael, you can learn some new tricks later today on the computer if you want."

But I wanted to know the tricks now, and I didn't.

The kids were all waiting and I didn't know how to be friends with them if I wasn't entertaining them.

I kept looking up at Ms. T because I knew that if I looked down, I would see disappointed faces, and I couldn't handle that. My eyes began to get blurry as tears began to fill them. I couldn't help it—a tear slipped down my cheek. I thought I would cry forever. The thought of crying forever made me continue to cry.

"It is okay, Michael. We can play other games," Henry said.

But I wanted to do another magic trick, and I could feel my face sink even further downward into one big clump of failure. I had let everyone down. I crossed my arms, mostly to hold my body still. I began to curl up into a ball. I didn't want anyone to see me, but everyone kept looking at me. I didn't know how to ask for space. I didn't know how to be sad and be okay at the same time. I didn't know a lot, and I was also only ten years old, so maybe that made sense?

Or maybe there was something deeply wrong with me. I was sad about not knowing another magic trick. I was sad the microwave was broken and we couldn't use it. I was sad about the math test that I didn't do well on, and that I couldn't understand math better, like some people. I was sad I didn't know a lot of things, like my teacher. She seemed to know everything.

The bell to go outside for lunch rang. Thankfully!

"Can everyone put their lunch kits in the cloak-room and head out for lunch? Michael, Jenni and Johnny, can you come to my desk, please?" said Ms. T, motioning with her hands for Johnny to come in from the hall.

Ms. T had a granola bar in her hand. It looked like the same one she had been holding since earlier that morning when we didn't listen to that story she was trying to read us. Had she been holding the same granola bar since early that morning?

That thought made me feel hungry. Maybe I was just tired? Maybe I was just sad. I didn't know what I was feeling—and that made me feel even more sad. Ms. T was always so polite and kind. She always spoke with nice words and was able to manage her emotions and knew everything. Maybe adults didn't have these kinds of troubles? Maybe when I became an adult, it would all go away? I walked slowly to Ms. T's desk with my head low and tears streaming

down my face. I didn't want to pour all of my emotions on her, but as soon as I got to her desk, I started crying, as hard as I had ever cried.

Then I noticed that Jenni stood shaking on the other side of Ms. T's desk, and she was shaking so much she made the floor and desk shake. Johnny ran in from the hallway, dropped to the floor and pounded his fists over and over on the carpet.

Ms. T's papers started to fly off her desk.

"YOU ALL NEED TO STOP," she shouted in frustration, but it was like we couldn't hear her.

I kept crying, Jenni kept shaking, Johnny kept banging his fists and the papers kept flying and swirling in all of the emotions.

Ms. T started to bite her lip and waved her hands in the air. "Please stop, please stop. All my things are going to get wrecked."

I could barely see because my eyes and mind were so blurry, but I watched the red bell with little white flowers, that once belonged to Ms. T's grandma, begin to fall. The bell moved as if it was in slow motion toward Ms. T's photo of her little pug puppy, Lucy.

Bling, Bling, ZIP, ZAP, ZOOP, POOF, KABAM, BEEP, BEEP!

Just then, Microwave Bling Bling's lights flashed and made weird noises. The last two piercing beeps made us all stop.

Ms. T grabbed the bell a millisecond before it would have broken the photo frame. She picked up both the bell and the frame, squeezing them to her heart.

We all looked at the microwave, mesmerized by the bright colours swirling around it and the bright, white light shining up toward the ceiling.

It was almost like the microwave was coming alive, with feet and legs and a personality.

For a moment, we all paused and forgot about everything that came before and everything that would come after.

We were just there, in that moment, no judgment. All the worries and thoughts in our heads disappeared.

Chapter 4
Microwave Bling Bling

"Bling Bling, Beep Beep," I said as I turned the window door of my stomach into a screen playing a video of everything that had happened earlier. It began with Johnny, beeping at the very moment when Johnny began to feel upset.

A few moments later, his eyes big with surprise, Johnny said, "Oh, I didn't even realize I stomped toward Microwave Bling Bling like that, or that I ripped open the door. I wish I would have paid attention to my feelings inside my body—maybe I could have paused, reset, taken a deep breath and asked for a break."

I continued to show Johnny, Jenni, Michael and Ms. T the rest of the scene. Real-life Johnny said, "Jenni, you asked how I was doing? And you too, Michael? I didn't know you both cared about me."

Jenni, forgetting her fear of sharing her emotions, said, "Of course, Johnny. You are one of my best friends!"

"Bling Bling, Beep Beep," I said.

The scene changed, and showed a boy that looked like Johnny, now bigger and in high school. He pushed over desks and kicked things, and the other students around him ran away, afraid of his anger. As the video continued, it was clear Johnny was alone and had no friends. No one understood what was going on for him. He felt bad, and everyone treated him as though he was bad.

"Oh no! I don't want people to be afraid of me like that," real-life Johnny burst out. "I want people to want to be my friends, like you, Jenni. I guess I need more tools to support me when I am angry and on the top of the emotion tree or to notice even before I get to the top of the emotion tree. I need to notice my emotions and to pause and ask for space to manage them."

"I wonder what that would look like?" Ms. T said.

"*Bling Bling. Beep Beep,*" I said.

In the video, the scene changed. It was Johnny, still in high school, but when something made him angry, he stopped—he paused.

He took a deep breath, and said, "I am feeling angry."

His friends and teachers seemed cool with him saying how he was feeling, nodding their heads and waiting for him to tell them what he needed. Most importantly, high-school Johnny seemed to accept all of his emotions. He asked for space out in the hall, and when he came back into class, people smiled at him. He felt accepted, and calm. High-school Johnny knew that, strangely, having quiet time alone when he needed it helped him feel less alone all the time. He didn't fight with his emotions anymore, because he knew feeling emotions is a healthy part of being human.

"Wow, it looks like I understand that I have many emotions, especially my go-to emotion, anger, and that it is okay," says real-life Johnny. "I can pay attention to my feelings, pause and ask for help when I need it."

He looked like he'd just discovered he had a superpower. And, in a way, he did!

Jenni appeared in the video next. Watching herself, she saw how she put her hand up, then took it down, and then put it up and took it down. She hid behind her hands, but was curious about what else my microwave screen had to show her. Jenni peeked through the space between her fingers. Finally, she began to peel away her hands, along with the feeling of needing to hide.

"I don't want to be so afraid all the time. I want to share. It is okay to share, right?" Jenni asked.

Johnny said, "Yes, I share my feelings all the time. Maybe I can give you a bit of my oversharing and I can take some of your not-sharing and then we can be balanced."

Jenni laughed out loud.

Jenni never laughed out loud. Sure, she had her nervous giggle, but no one had ever heard her big belly laugh. It was great!

Johnny, Michael and Ms. T laughed too. It was a nice feeling.

I also laughed with them, but it was a very low laugh.

No one noticed, which was probably good, because a laughing microwave might be a bit surprising.

"Bling Bling, Beep Beep," I said.

The video moved over to high-school Jenni. She seemed so nervous and had long hair that she hid behind, hanging around in the hallway like she was afraid to go to class. She chewed on her nails and had short, frantic breathing. Then the video showed her hanging out with kids that were drawing all over themselves with markers. Jenni did it too, even though it looked like she didn't want to.

Real-life Jenni blurted, "I don't want to do things just because other people want me to. I want to do things because I want to, in my heart. I have to learn how to speak up. My voice matters, right? I matter, right? I need to find more tools to help me get over my fears. Maybe I can just try to speak a bit more, like I am now. Nothing bad is happening!"

Jenni told everyone about how she'd spoken up in class in grade one and was told it wasn't time to talk. "I thought that meant that it was never a good time for me to speak. But maybe my teacher just meant it was just not a good time at that moment?"

Michael, Johnny, Ms. T and I all nodded our heads enthusiastically, feeling thankful for being there for Jenni's breakthrough.

Encouraged, she said, "I don't want to be afraid of everything. What does it look like to be brave and confident, I wonder?"

"Bling Bling, Beep Beep," I said.

The video went back to Jenni in high school, but this time, she was in class, listening to her teacher before putting her hand up and going to the front of the class to share her project. She seemed to glow from head to toe, and held her head high. Not in a rude way, but in a brave, confident, kind way. This Jenni met her friends in the hallway after class, hugging them and being hugged back. When she didn't feel comfortable doing something, she said, politely and respectfully, "No, I don't want to." Instead, she did the things her heart felt called to do, like reading and writing—even sharing her work in front of the class.

She knew she would probably always have some fear, but she knew she could work through it, talking to her teachers and friends and to a counsellor when needed.

Michael appeared in the video next, sitting on the carpet showing magic tricks. He was upset, and as people tried to come up to him, he turned his back and wouldn't let anyone close.

"Oh no, I am turning my back on people, but all I really want is to feel close. I can see that I am the reason that I feel alone," Michael said.

"Bling Bling, Beep Beep," I said.

Next, the video showed high-school Michael, bigger and older but still looking sad and isolating himself from the other kids.

One of the kids said, "I really like being around Michael, but he always pushes me away."

"He pushes me away too. I think Michael is the best, but I can't always try to be his friend if he pushes me away," said another.

"Bling Bling, Beep Beep," I said.

"I never hear nice things people say like this when I'm sad," real-life Michael said. "I only hear, 'you aren't funny, you don't know enough magic tricks, you aren't good enough.' But I guess NO ONE is actually saying that—I made it all up in my head."

Jenni said, "Maybe you can pay attention when you start to feel sad and say nice things to yourself, like 'I am okay, people like me,' instead of the negative chatter."

"Yes—if I can make up negative things and believe them, I am sure I could make up positive things and believe them too," said Michael, laughing a bit.

"Michael, what do you think it would look like if you believed positive things about yourself?" Ms. T said.

"Bling Bling, Beep Beep," I said.

The video went back to high-school Michael and instead Michael used his words to communicate and believed people liked him. High-school Michael stood by high-school Jenni's desk and said, "I feel sad that you don't want to see my new magic trick, but it is okay, I know you want to eat."

"Of course, I want to see your magic trick! Can I see it after I am done eating? We can practice for your magic show," Jenni said.

Michal smiled and said, "Sure!"

"Bling Bling, Beep Beep," I said.

Everyone smiled at all of the videos of the past and the future. Everyone felt happy that they might still all be friends in high school, and they had learned something important about focusing on all the things that went right, instead of focusing on the things that didn't.

"Bling Bling, Beep Beep," I said.

I was happy too, as reflecting back on everyone's emotions allowed me to know that we all have emotions, even me, Microwave Bling Bling. I learned that my grounded level is my reset button. At this grounded level of zero, I am just being me and able to connect to myself and with others. Sometimes when I am off the grounded level for too long, I can feel very out of control, so much that I can shut right down, which is what happened today. I don't want to shut down, because I really love connecting to myself and others, especially this class, but my system can be so overwhelmed that there is a system overload. It is my job to recognize and notice when I am off the grounded level for too long. It is my job to use my emotional backpack of tools and ask for help. I can let the class know with a beep beep that I need a break. Even though I cannot talk like humans, I can still communicate with beeps and flashes, and I will do that more.

Chapter 5
Ms. T

I appeared in the video and the kids all looked at me closely with surprise.

"Wait, Ms. T, you have emotions too?" Johnny asked.

I smiled. "Johnny, we all have emotions. Just because I am an adult doesn't mean I don't have emotional things I am working on too. In fact, as an adult, the emotions I didn't learn to manage when I was your age have become patterns, and so they're even harder to deal with."

"Like what?" asked Jenni. "What kind of patterns?"

"Such as the pattern of wanting to always fix every-one around me and forgetting to take care of myself,"

I said, holding up my still uneaten granola bar and laughing.

Next, we watched the video of me earlier in the day.

"Bling Bling, Beep Beep," said Microwave Bling Bling.

"In the video, I can see that I tried to eat lunch, but everyone else's needs seemed more important, and I kept getting up and forgetting about my food. I got hungrier and hungrier, and then the yelling happened.

"I can see that I hadn't eaten all day—I forgot to take care of me, so I could not take care of all of you with kindness. Some adults call that, 'giving from an empty cup,' and then I yelled," I explained.

"What could you have done differently?" asked Johnny. "I mean, you're the teacher—you have to take care of us, right?"

"I should have asked for help from another teacher. I have to break my patterns and remind myself it is okay to ask for help. Or I could have just asked all of you to give me a minute because I needed to eat too," I replied.

"Bling Bling, Beep Beep," said Microwave

Bling Bling.

The scene changed to the classroom five years later. I was teaching kids but I looked a lot older and weak. I yelled at everyone and I was on my phone asking artificial intelligence for ways to find new jobs and retire early.

"I cannot continue to put myself second, or I won't be able to do this job anymore. I love this job! I love working with all of you. I need to press the reset button and pause when everything is overwhelming. I need to put my hand on my heart and ask myself what I need, which is usually food. I then need to take care of that need right away," I said.

"And what does that look like, if you meet your own needs first?" asked Jenni.

"Bling Bling, Beep Beep," said Microwave Bling Bling.

The scene changed to five years later, but I almost looked five years younger. I asked for what I needed and took the time to eat and meet my needs. The class was independent and everyone worked as a team, rather than relying completely on one person to solve every problem.

"Ms. T, I am sorry all of us took all of your time

today," Johnny said. Jenni and Michael nodded in agreement.

"Thanks, Johnny, but you don't need to be sorry. It is my job to handle my own emotions. I am sorry that I didn't take time for myself so I could be at my best for all of you. I will do better at that and remind myself that taking care of myself is self-love, and not selfish," I replied.

"I will do better at noticing my anger in my body and opening up my emotional backpack parachute quicker, using my tools, such as asking for a break," Johnny said.

"I will do better at taking a deep breath and speaking up even when I am feeling scared," Jenni said.

"I will do better at noticing when I am letting sadness get the best of me, and focus my attention on positive thoughts and all the good things around me," Michael said.

Chapter 6

Jenni

"BLING, BLING, BLING, ZIP, ZAP, ZOOP, Beep, Beep, Beep," said Microwave Bling Bling.

I laughed and laughed, more than I had laughed in a very long time, and I wasn't afraid to laugh or be myself anymore.

"I like your laugh," Johnny said and he laughed with me too.

Colours began to swirl all around the room, the lights began to blink and the microwave came back to full life. It was almost like Microwave Bling Bling was agreeing with all that we had just learned. Learning these lessons made us rich; we had Microwave Bling Bling to thank for that. I smiled at Microwave Bling Bling, and for a moment, it looked like Microwave Bling Bling's legs were in a criss-crossed meditative pose with Microwave Bling Bling smiling back at us saying, "Calm begins within me." We all began saying it too.

"Calm begins within me, calm begins within me."

We all took a deep breath in and deep breath out while pressing each finger one at a time to our thumbs as we said the words, "Calm begins within me."

And we all looked at each other and smiled. It was our responsibility to press our own pause button to reset to the calm within. It was our own responsibility to recognize the emotions in our body before climbing up the emotion tree. It was our responsibility to open up our emotional backpack to find and use our tools to parachute back down to a grounded level.

In this pause with the microwave showing us a rewind of our days and what the future may look like, we were able to be in connection with ourselves and at the same time be in connection with one another. I had never felt more connected to myself or others, and I knew that it was in the pauses

of life, the pressing of the reset button, where I could notice what was going on within my body and use my tools, such as deep breaths, positive thoughts, accepting myself and emotions, saying phrases or words such as, "Calm begins within me," and visualizing the things I want. These tools would help me feel grounded.

"I am thankful that all of these connections were allowed to form today," I said with confidence.

Johnny, Michael, Ms. T and even Microwave Bling Bling looked like they all nodded in agreement.

Chapter 7
Johnny

The lunch bell rang and all of the students came back into the classroom.

Ms. T said for the afternoon we were going to move our bodies and have a dance party.

Everyone cheered.

I think I cheered the loudest. My mouth kept pulling upright and the edges of my mouth wouldn't go down.

I think that was what a perma-grin felt like and you know what?

It felt amazing.

My eyes felt like they were in a dream, a happy dream, solid on a grounded level.

The rest of the class hadn't just learned all of the things we learned, but our positive energy radiated out to them too—just as Microwave Bling Bling had transformed its heating waves into positive energy that radiated out to us. I knew that anytime I looked at or thought of Microwave Bling Bling, I could remember these lessons, pause, reset, and radiate positive vibes to myself and to others. I could feel calm within at any time, or ask for support when I couldn't.

We danced, sang and had fun, including Ms. T. This may have been my imagination, but it was like Microwave Bling Bling really came to life. It felt like

Microwave Bling Bling was the DJ to our dance party with Kevin and Linda, our eraser friends, as the back-up dancers. This Tuesday was one of the best. It changed all of the Tuesdays moving forward. Did we still have emotions? Of course, we did, but we got better at recognizing our emotions earlier, pressing the reset button, pausing, and using our tools to manage ourselves.

And, on Tuesdays, we were calm.

CYNTHIA BERENYI lives in Victoria, B.C. where she incorporates mindfulness practices into her elementary school teaching position. She has created a mindfulness program that aligns with her research for her master's degree project investigating mindfulness techniques to enhance learning, development and well-being for children. She hopes her research and additional learning resources can provide valuable tools and insights to support the potential benefits of integrating social-emotional and mindfulness techniques within the education system. Cynthia is working on her third book and when she is not teaching or writing, she enjoys time with her family, friends, and with her puppy out in nature.

Acknowledgments

This book was created with the support of so many people and I am so thankful to everyone who has supported me and the unfolding of this book.

I wish to acknowledge and honour the traditional territory of the Coast Salish people, where I live, work, study, play and write.

I wish to acknowledge Canada as my homeland and Hungary as my parents' homeland, and the honour to have both Canadian and Hungarian nationalities.

Thank you to all the students who have enriched my life over the last 15-plus years, especially my 2022-2023 DIV 3 class, who taught me the most about mindfulness and the importance of taking pauses throughout the day.

Thank you to the two students who inspired the Kevin and Linda eraser characters and the creative magic that came from those students and characters.

Thank you to my new DIV 1 class of 2023 for supporting this new book and this creative journey.

Thank you to Lori Bamber for editing this book, even during retirement. I am always honoured to work with you and appreciate your insights and how you always have the perfect wording for creating a heartfelt emotion.

Thank you to Elise for all your attention to detail in the final edits of this book. I appreciate your expertise and efficiency.

Thank you, Stephen and Kevin, my illustrators, for making these characters come to life, especially Microwave Bling Bling. Your illustrations created the magic of this book.

Thank you, Kristy Twellmann Hill, my designer, for bringing this whole project together and reminding me of the joys of working as a team and creating books. I appreciate you.

Thank you, Andrew Ramirez, Heidi Cook, Anna

Mullen, Megan and The Self Publishing Agency, for always creating places that bring writers together and people whom I can go to for writing support.

Thank you Lisa Baylis, Stephanie Curran, Jonni-Lyn Friel and Cynthia Wong for teaching me about the power of the heart and mind connection through yoga and mindfulness.

Thank you to all of the master's degree teachers from Yorkville University who supported my research journey on investigating mindfulness and who all reminded me of the importance of education, learning and discovering new insights.

Thank you to all my teaching friends, educational support staff, counsellors and administrative staff who constantly inspire me with the work they do with children each day.

Thank you to all my teachers, especially Mr. Pernu, who made school and learning fun!

Thank you to my friends for always supporting my writing journey and my creative side. I appreciate sharing all the stages of my journey with you.

Thank you to my grandparents, especially Grandma who always taught me to be me.

Thank you, brother; who I shared a range of emotions and many childhood memories with.

Thank you, mom; you are my mom, and more importantly my friend. I appreciate your love and support and the way we continue to grow in our mother/daughter relationship.

Thank you, dad; you were always my solid rock and a solid friend when you were on this earth. I appreciate the wisdom, support and love that still fill my heart in remembrance of your essence. You will always be my best friend.

Thank you to the reader; I hope this book gives you a sense of calm and support throughout this amazing magical journey of emotions and life.

Resources

Enhance the magic of *On Tuesdays We Are Wild: Mindfulness Adventures with Microwave Bling Bling* with our fantastic teaching and parenting resources!

For valuable tools and materials that make mindfulness learning a breeze, visit the website below:

www.calmbegins.com

www.mindfulnessmermaidpublishing.com